T0089195

Design, snip, clip . . .

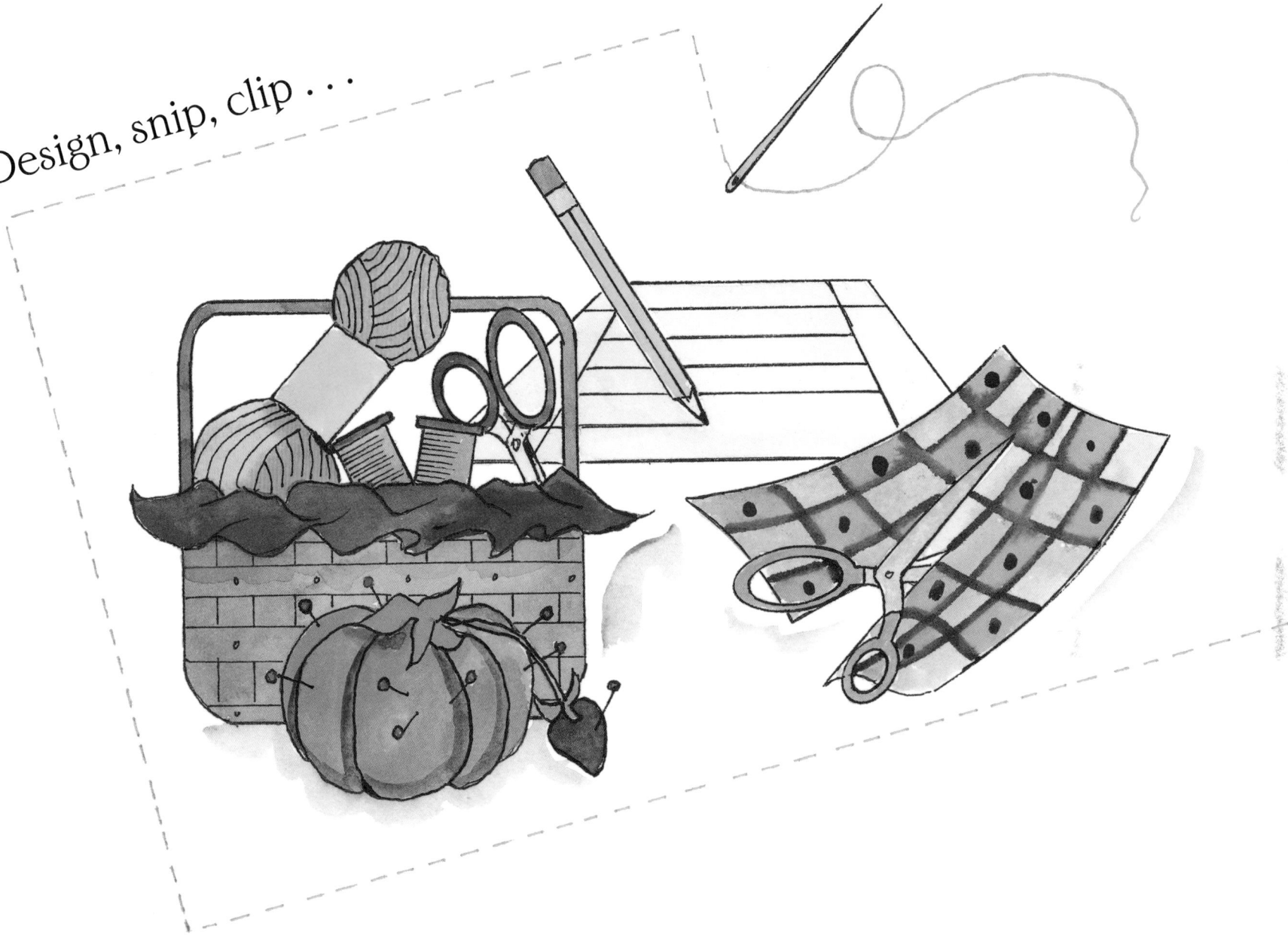

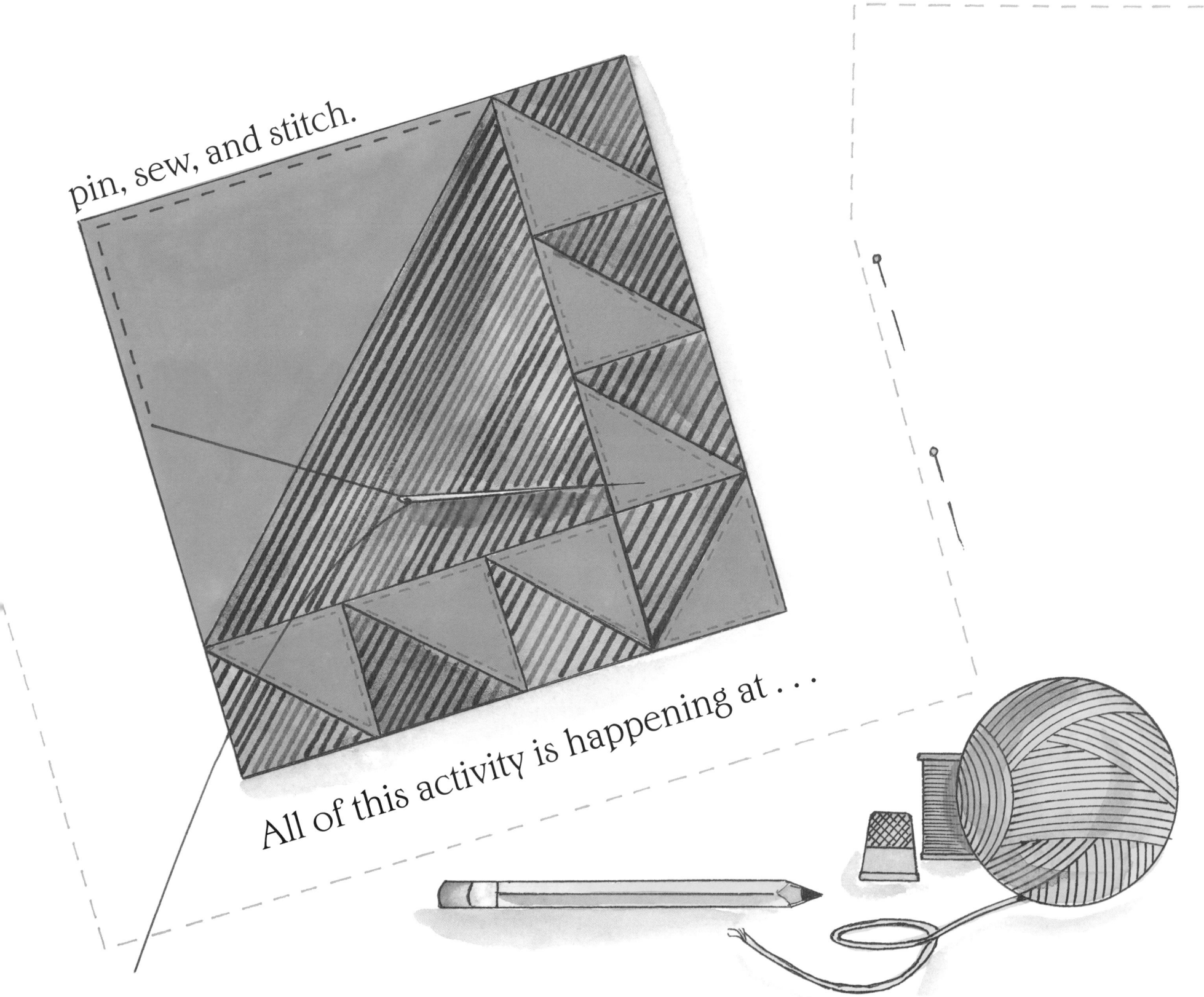
pin, sew, and stitch.
All of this activity is happening at . . .

The Quilting Bee

by Gail Gibbons

HarperCollins*Publishers*

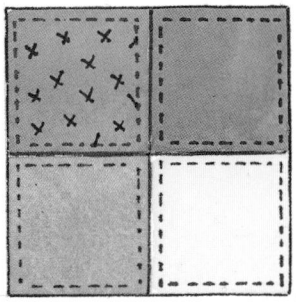

Special thanks to
Louise Young of East Corinth, Vermont,
for her expert advice on quilt making.
Also, I want to thank Eula Stevens
for the lovely quilt she made for me.

The Quilting Bee
Copyright © 2004 by Gail Gibbons
Printed in the United States of America. All rights reserved.
www.harperchildrens.com

Library of Congress Cataloging-in-Publication Data
Gibbons, Gail.
The quilting bee / by Gail Gibbons.
p. cm.
Summary: An introduction to the process of quilt making, including a history of the craft, sample quilt patterns, and directions for creating a children's book authors' and illustrators' quilt.
ISBN 0-688-16397-1 — ISBN 0-688-16398-X (lib. bdg.)
1. Patchwork—United States—Patterns—Juvenile literature. 2. Patchwork quilts—United States—History—Juvenile literature. 3. Quilting—United States—Societies, etc.—Juvenile literature. [1. Patchwork. 2. Quilting. 3. Quilts. 4. Handicraft.] I. Title.
TT835 .G527 2004 746.46—dc21 2002023310

Typography by Jeanne L. Hogle
21 22 PC 20
❖
First Edition

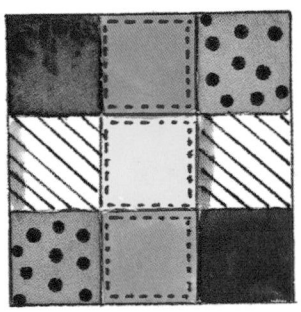

QUILT MAKING REQUIRES ADULT SUPERVISION.

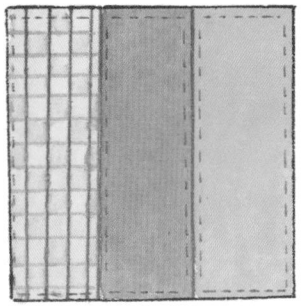

Because bees are good at working together, the word *bee* came to mean people getting together to do some useful work. Have you ever heard of a *spelling bee*?

A group of quilt makers have come together to share their time and many talents piecing together a beautiful quilt. Their group is called a *quilting bee*, or a *quilting circle*.

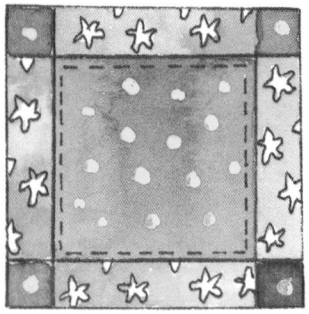

A quilt is a warm bed covering made up of three layers. There's the top layer that usually has a colorful design, the cotton padding in between, and the quilt's backing.

TOP LAYER

PADDING

BACKING

The word *quilt* comes from the Latin word *culcita,* which means "stuffed sack, mattress, or cushion."

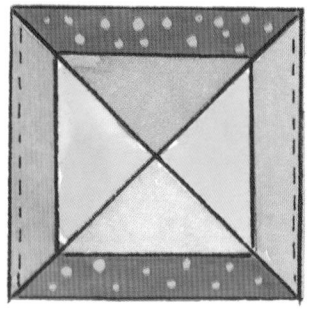

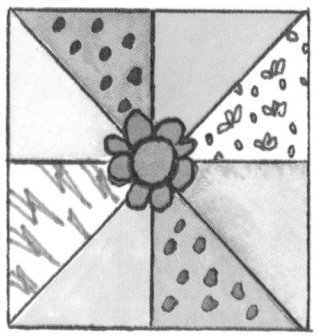

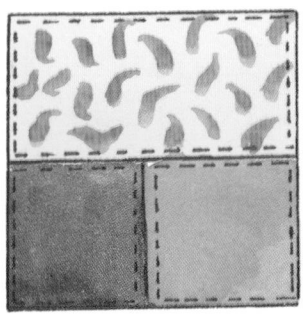

The quilters begin their project by carefully choosing, or designing themselves, a pattern for their quilt. Fabrics of different colors, textures, and patterns soon fill the room.

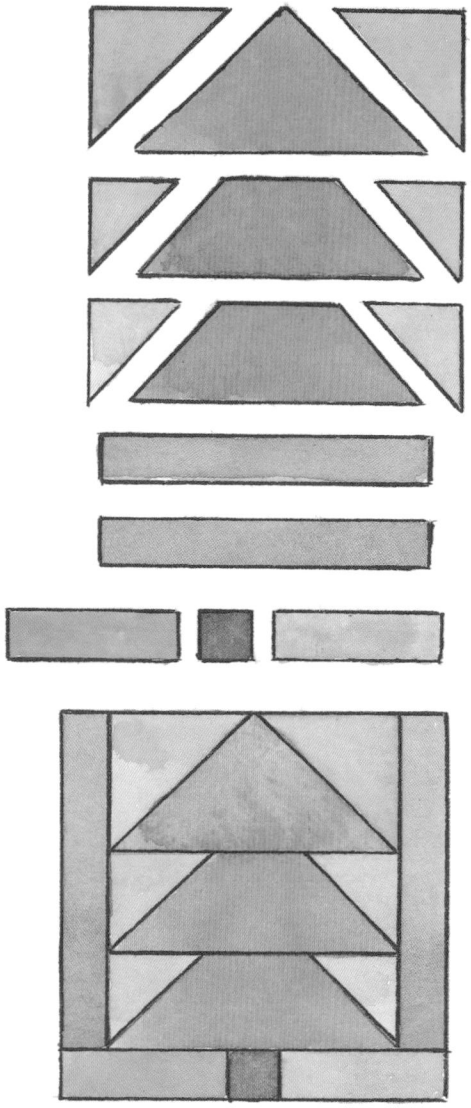

PINE TREE QUILT BLOCK

The quilters pick and choose the different fabrics they will use. They cut squares, triangles, and other shapes. Then they stitch the shapes together to make patterned squares called *quilt blocks.*

It takes a long time and many gatherings to create all the quilt blocks they will need. Finally the group begins to sew the blocks together. When they are done, they have a beautiful top layer for their quilt.

The top layer, the padding, and the material for the back of the quilt are stretched over a *quilting frame*. The quilters busy themselves stitching and tying the three layers together, using heavy thread or yarn.

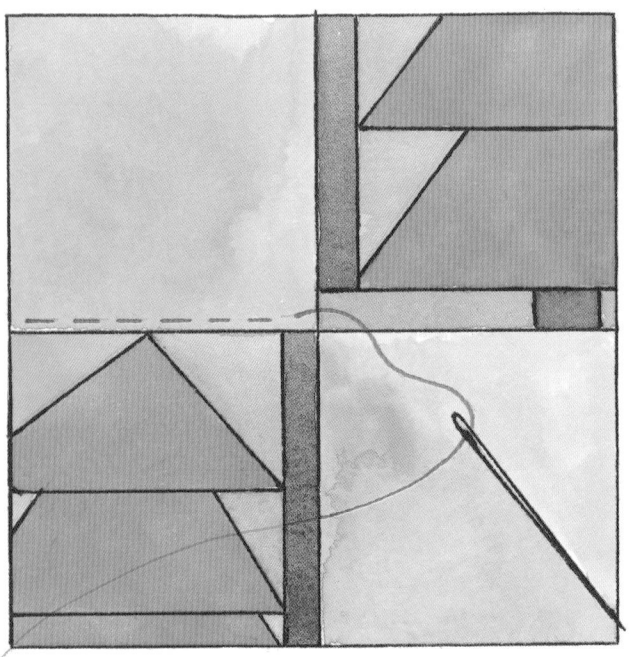

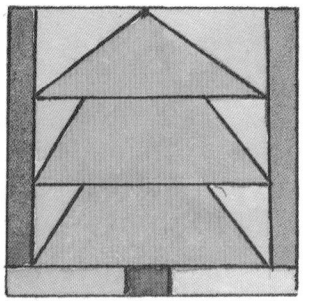

Over time the quilt begins to take shape. The room is full of activity. As the quilters stitch, they talk about the news and what's going on in their town.

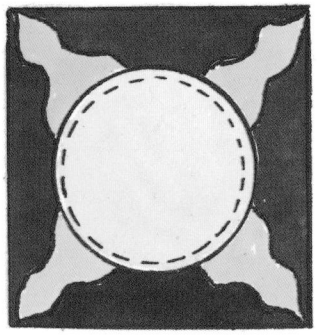

The art of quilting goes far back in time. The Egyptians, Chinese, and Turkish people used quilted material in their clothing for warmth. Quilting was also used as a cushion for heavy armor.

FOUR-PATCH block

NINE-PATCH block

The TRIP AROUND THE WORLD pattern was made up of tiny squares of fabric sewn together around one square.

In the United States pioneer women created quilts to keep their families cozy and warm. The simplest quilt blocks were usually the most popular designs for everyday use.

ALBUM QUILT blocks were signed in India ink or embroidery and given as gifts to a special friend or beloved family member.

Sometimes SIGNATURE QUILTS were made to be signed by famous people.

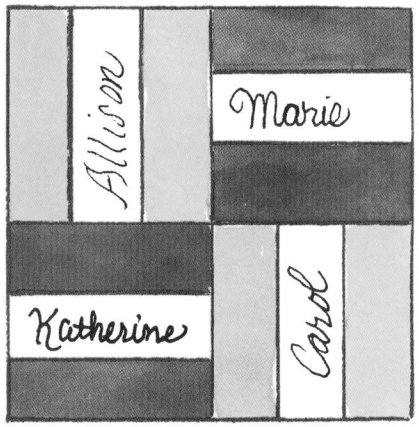

Pioneer families were very proud of their quilts. They created them from precious scraps of cloth. Quilts were made for all sorts of reasons.

Many quilt patterns had special stories to tell, such as what pioneers saw and felt as they traveled west.

The ROAD TO CALIFORNIA pattern looks like a wagon trail. It is also called the TRAIL OF THE COVERED WAGON.

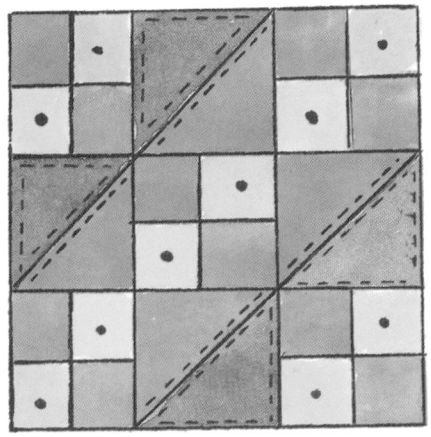

The HILL AND VALLEY quilt shows the land the pioneers passed through along the journey.

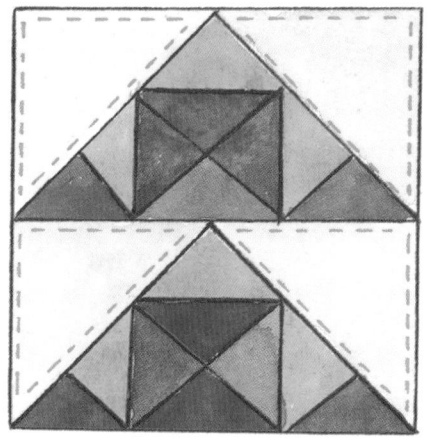

The ROCKY GLEN quilt shows the rough trails the pioneers had to struggle through.

BEAR'S PAW

HOVERING HAWKS

Many quilt patterns represented wild animals.

On the DOVE IN THE WINDOW quilt, doves seem to be touching their beaks in the center.

What are the creatures in the FISH pattern doing?

The pattern in the WATERWHEEL quilt is a reminder of the millstones used to grind grain.

RAIL FENCE

LOG CABIN

The LITTLE RED SCHOOLHOUSE design came from the one-room schoolhouses children attended.

Pioneer families often made quilts that reminded them of their new homes.

The BABY'S BLOCKS pattern looks like the simple toys that babies played with.

The KITCHEN WOOD BOX quilt reminded early Americans of the wood boxes they stored their firewood in for cooking and warmth.

The FRUIT BASKET quilt celebrated harvesttime.

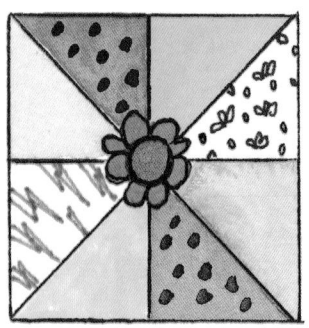

Other quilt designs reflect family life in the settlers' homes.

WEDDING RING design

FLOWERPOT design

The FRIENDSHIP RING quilt got its name because it took a ring of friends to gather the wide variety of fabrics needed to create it. This design is also known as the ASTER or DRESDEN PLATE.

The GRANDMA'S FAN pattern reminded families of their grandmother keeping cool on hot summer days.

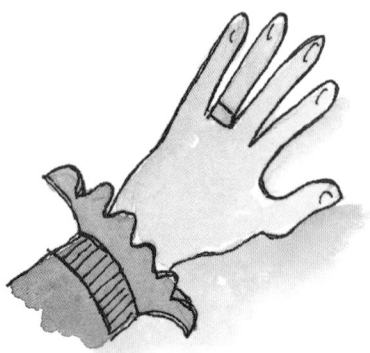

Many quilts expressed love and caring for other people.

OCEAN WAVES design

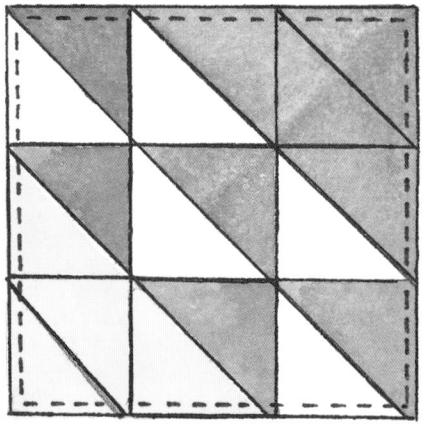

The NORTH WIND pattern looks like the wind moving across the prairie.

Weather played an important role in the everyday life of settlers, as was often seen in their quilt designs.

The WHIRLWIND design shows another kind of weather.

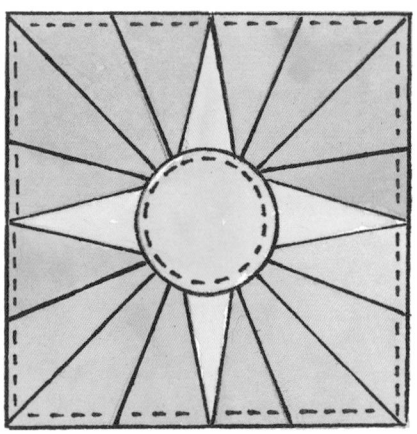

The SUNBURST design says "sunny day"!

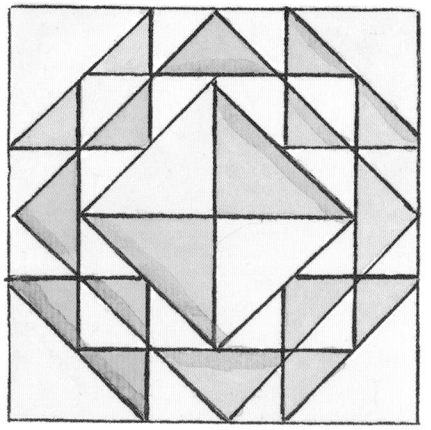

CORN AND BEANS quilt

NOONDAY LILY

HOLLYHOCK WREATH

In the GRAPE BASKET design the purple color in each basket represents harvested grapes.

Many traditional quilt patterns reflect the foods planted by the early Americans. Others represent the flowers they loved to grow.

BEAUTIFUL STAR

EIGHT-POINTED STAR

MILKY WAY

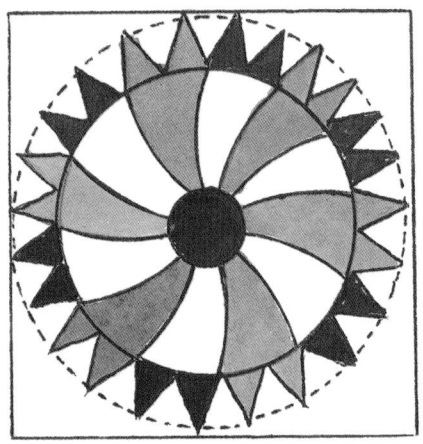

RISING SUN

Many quilt patterns were created from images of the stars of the night sky . . . and, in the morning, the rising sun.

One traditional pattern is called the *crazy quilt*. These quilts had no special pattern. Instead, many shapes and sizes of fabric were stitched together willy-nilly.

In the past, quilts could only be sewn by hand.

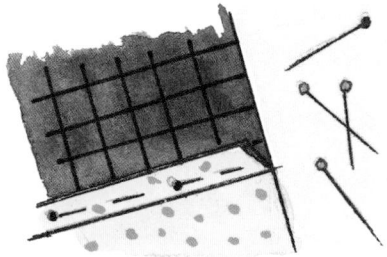

PINS held the fabric together before sewing.

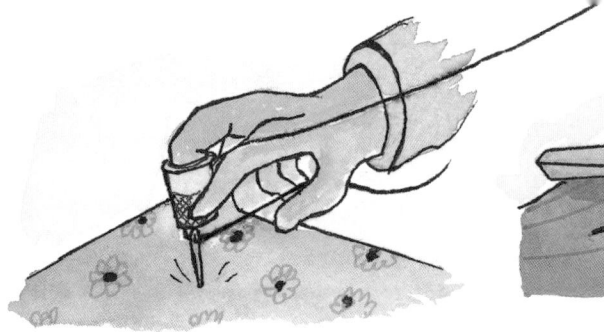

A THIMBLE protected the finger that pushed the NEEDLE through the fabric.

A SCISSORS was used to cut fabric.

A QUILTING FRAME held the quilt's three layers in place while they were stitched together.

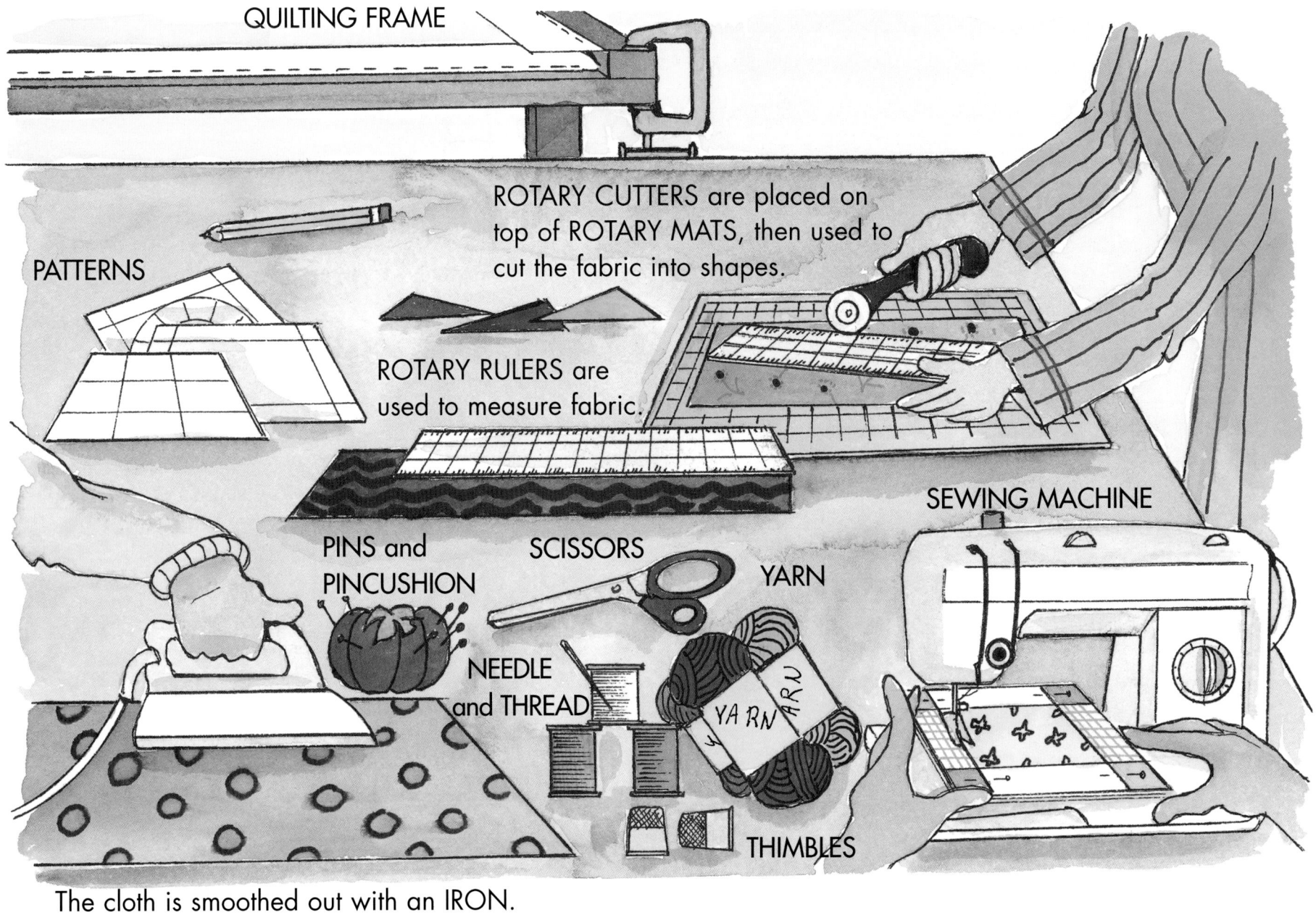

Today, at the quilting bee, the quilt makers use many modern tools to create their quilts and many tools that are familiar.

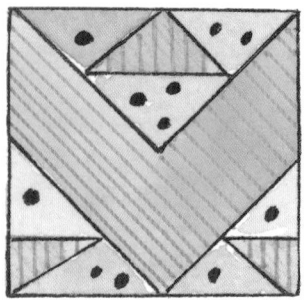

Today there are still county fairs, quilt shows, and contests to choose the most beautiful, original, and interesting quilt. Members of the sewing bee work hard so they can enter their quilt in a local contest.

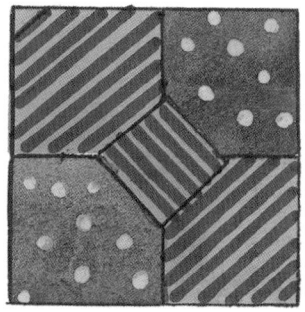

All around the different stands, quilts are on display. Some have traditional patterns; others are not traditional at all!

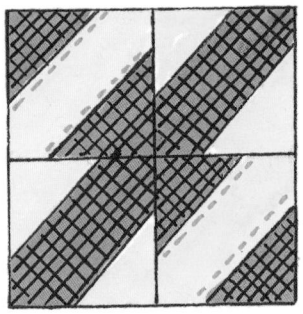

Judges walk by. They take notes, then cluster together to discuss the many quilt designs. The judges want to select a quilt that is truly special.

The judges have made up their minds. They gather in front of the quilting bee and award its entry first place. Quilters agree that the quilt is special because so much good talk, laughter, and friendship were sewn into it. Everyone applauds.

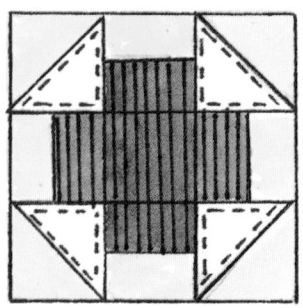

In a few weeks the quilting bee is at it again. . . .

An Authors' and Illustrators' Quilt

These students are planning a quilt project. They choose their favorite authors and illustrators and send each one a square cloth with a letter that describes the quilt project.

Most authors and illustrators are happy to join the project. They sign their names and sometimes make a drawing or a painting on the piece of cloth.

Then they send their quilt squares back to the students.

When all the squares are returned, adults help the students stitch them together into their very own authors' and illustrators' quilt. How special it is!

Design . . . Cut . . . Stitch . . .

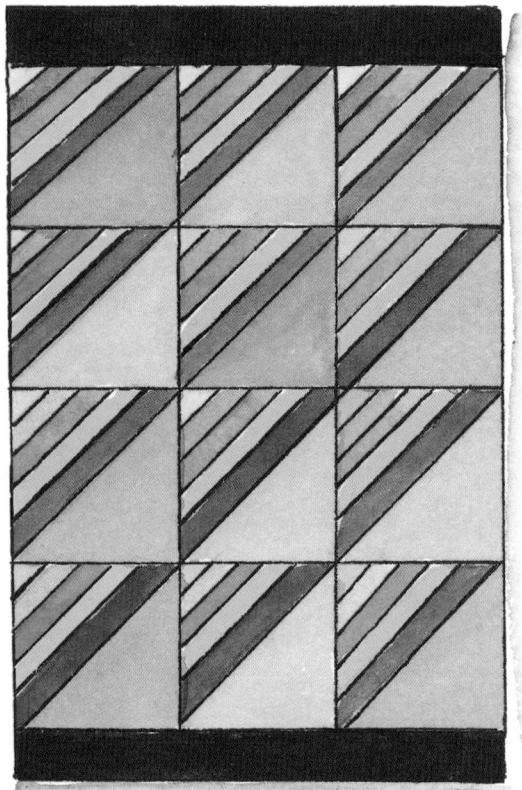

The Amish, a religious group, came to America to create their own farming communities. They are famous for their beautiful traditional quilts.

There are hundreds of traditional quilt designs.

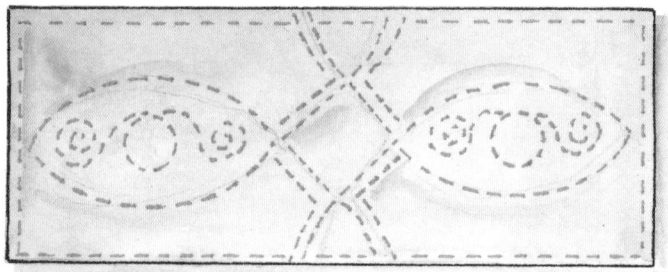

Often quilt makers decorate their quilts by doing fancy stitching on the top.

The TREE OF LIFE is an old colonial pattern. Often it was designed to represent a *family tree.* A family tree shows past and present members of a family.

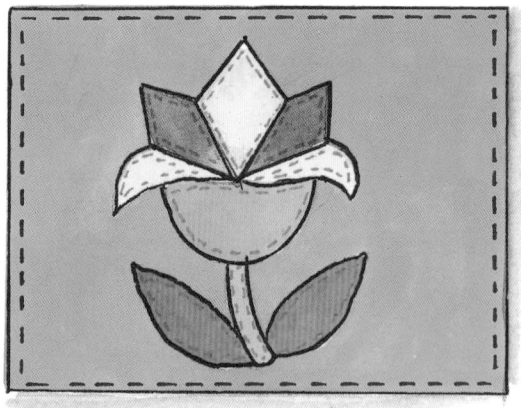

Sometimes APPLIQUÉ is used in quilting. That is when a piece of one fabric is sewn on top of another.

Today quilt makers use their imagination to create designs that are works of art.